July is National Blueberries Month.

Blueberry Picking

Can you find these hidden objects?

duck

teacup

boot

mushroom

fish

turtle

dragonfly

candle

golf club

strawberry

tack

handbell

canoe

funnel

ice-cream cone

frog

Ring-Tailed Lemurs

bowl

heart

dog bone

glove

bell

jump rope

spoon

walnut

shuttlecock

sailboat

crescent moon

paper airplane

Can you find these hidden objects?

Highlights®

Artist Michelangelo began work on the Sistine Chapel in 1508 — 500 years ago.

bunch of bananas

duck

hot dog

safety pin

clothespin

chameleon

hockey stick

spoon

Can you find these hidden objects?

rabbit

mushroom

lipstick

bowling pin

hammer

mop

penguin

Fishing from the Bridge

mushroom

tack

candle

mitten

ballpoint pen

radish

Can you find these hidden objects?

shoe

pencil

bell

musical note

ice-cream cone

spoon

Highlights®

Being Neighborly

ruler

bird

pliers

stamp

feather

hat

caterpillar

Can you find these hidden objects?

tweezers

eyeglasses

button

wishbone

heart

hockey stick

Play Ball!

ghost

glove

cupcake

nail

cat's head

pencil

Can you find these hidden objects?

worm

domino

snowcone

fish

mouse

slice of pizza

Highlights®

snake

mug

pennant

slice of pie

banana

sock

kite

sailboat

ice-cream bar

spool of thread

bowl

golf club

candle

button

flowerpot

Can you find these hidden objects?

Illustrated by David Helton

A Drive in the Country

flag

crutch

toothbrush

ladle

needle

golf club

golf tee

earmuffs

Can you find these hidden objects?

mitten

toy top

teacup

pennant

penguin

chili pepper

pencil

caterpillar

sock

Illustrated by Elizabeth Allyn

Highlights®

Washington Irving, who wrote *The Legend of Sleepy Hollow*, was born 225 years ago in 1783.

fish

bottle

toothbrush

banana

bat

spoon

heart

artist's brush

carrot

bell

glove

sailboat

Can you find these hidden objects?

Fun at the Fair

sock

closed umbrella

needle

bell

slice of pizza

fish

musical note

Can you find these hidden objects?

heart

caterpillar

tack

worm

eyeglasses

spool of thread

mushroom

comb

swim fin

Highlights®

pickle

snake

jump rope

tent

fish

sailboat

candle

needle

bowl

heart

baseball bat

mouse

Can you find these hidden objects?

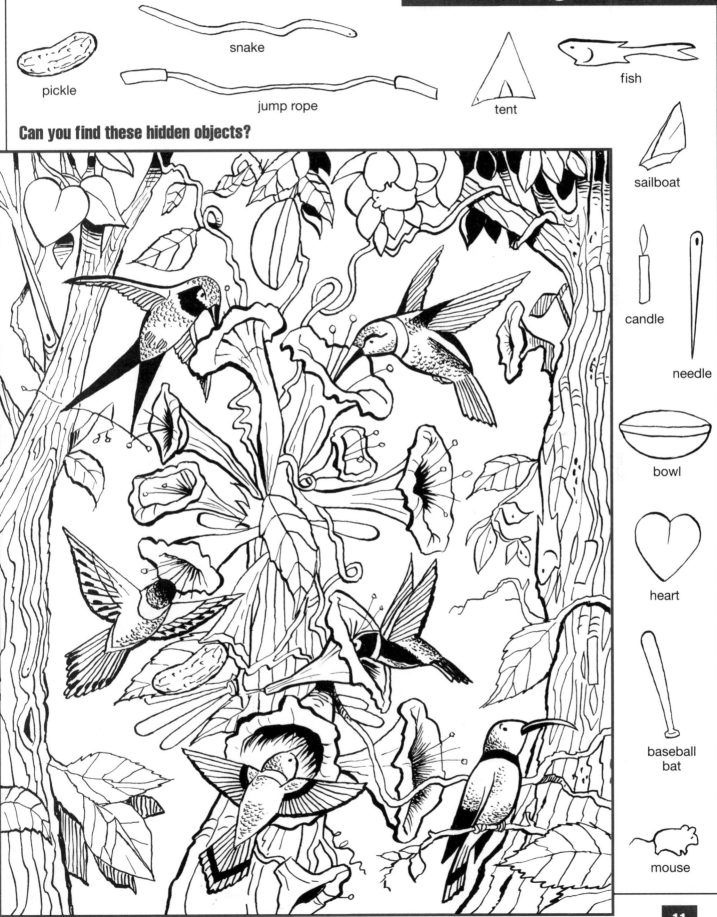

insect

party hat

candle

squeeze bottle

ring

drinking glass

trowel

nail

witch's hat

Can you find these hidden objects?

fish

tweezers

seal

flag

mushroom

needle

snake

artist's brush

chili pepper

PUPPET SHOW

The first pencil with an attached eraser was patented 150 years ago in 1858.

pliers

lightning bolt

snail

Can you find these hidden objects?

sailboat

toothbrush

party hat

spoon

baseball bat

crescent moon

pennant

needle

envelope

ring

hockey stick

football

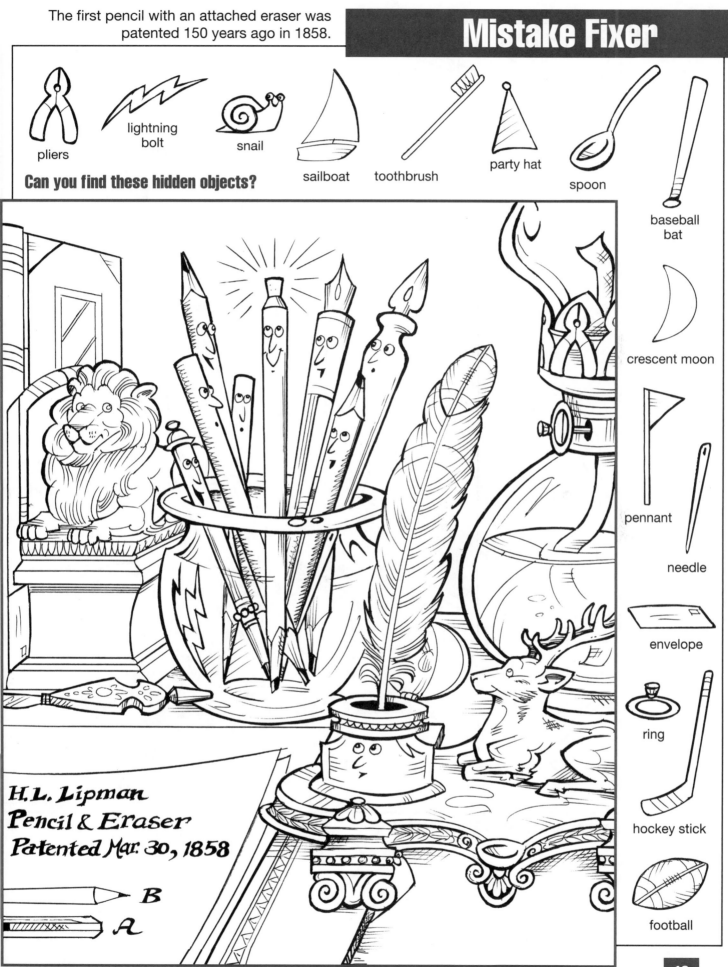

H.L. Lipman
Pencil & Eraser
Patented Mar. 30, 1858

B

A

www.Highlights.com

Underwater Tunnel

The first tunnel under the Hudson River opened in 1908—100 years ago.

flag

needle

crayon

sailboat

flashlight

Can you find these hidden objects?

ladle

bowl

top hat

ice-cream bar

heart

slice of pie

sock

slice of pizza

Highlights®

Can you find these hidden objects?

crown

toothbrush

musical note

drinking straw

tack

slice of cake

pennant

artist's brush

golf club

ice-cream cone

hockey stick

sock

needle

baseball cap

slipper

slice of bread

apple core

flag

ring

ladle

toothbrush

iron

seashell

Can you find these hidden objects?

rolling pin

safety pin

baseball cap

mushroom

boomerang

scissors

Picnic on the Porch

Can you find these hidden objects?

ice-cream cone
ruler
hat
slice of pie
telescope
tack
toothbrush
canoe
ring
crown
mallet
spoon
sailboat
musical note
candle
artist's brush
mushroom

Scouting Begins

coat hanger

ice-cream cone

crescent moon

wristwatch

saw

banana

fish

worm

CAMPING

WOODCRAFT

AQUATICS

Can you find these hidden objects?

rabbit

hatchet

carrot

fork

nail

bug

paper clip

Highlights®

1908
Scouting Movement Founded
ROBERT BADEN POWELL

SPORTS

Backpacking AND HiKING

sock

piece of candy corn

candle

golf club

cane

needle

cotton swab

moccasin

porcupine

rocket ship

crown

slice of pizza

snake

Illustrated by Apryl Stott

19

At the Dentist

Lucy Hobbs Taylor, the first woman to receive a degree in dentistry, was born 175 years ago.

crayon

ring

pencil

arrow

spool of thread

nail

toothbrush

Can you find these hidden objects?

open book

teacup

bell

leaf

iron

crescent moon

seashell

fishhook

comb

Highlights®

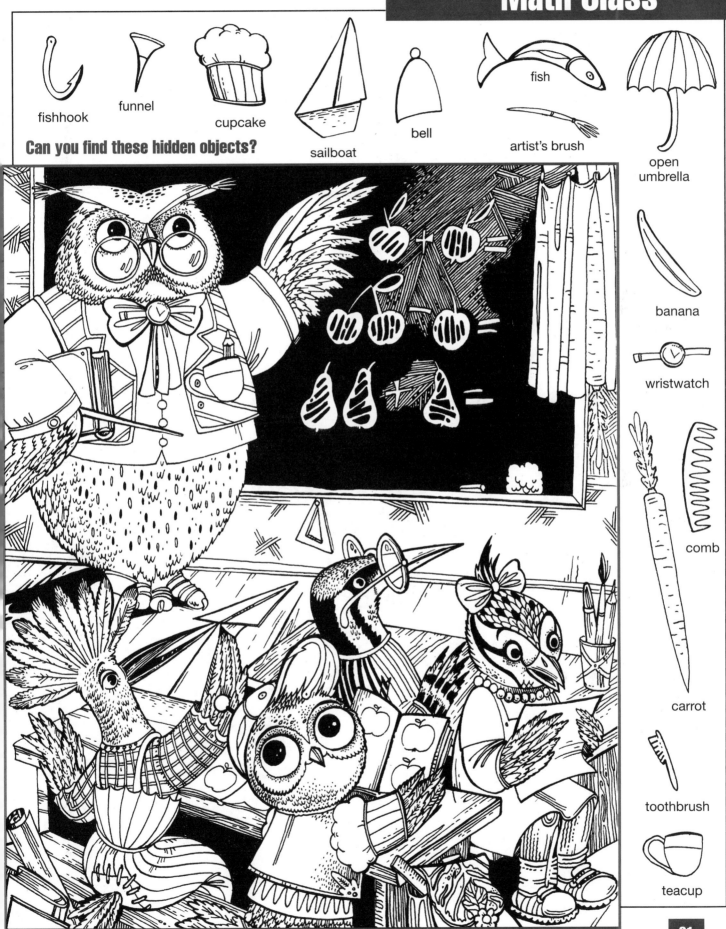

fishhook

funnel

cupcake

Can you find these hidden objects?

sailboat

bell

fish

artist's brush

open umbrella

banana

wristwatch

comb

carrot

toothbrush

teacup

Dingoes Down Under

slice of pie

fishhook

needle

top hat

flag

turnip

slice of pizza

snake

caterpillar

heart

hairbrush

fish

Can you find these hidden objects?

Highlights®

The Morning Rush

banana

saltshaker

feather

mushroom

needle

heart

mallet

ring

Can you find these hidden objects?

golf club

toothbrush

tack

pencil

flashlight

tube of toothpaste

23

Washday Wonder

The first electric washing machine was introduced 100 years ago.

pencil

wishbone

mug

pennant

sailboat

fishhook

drinking straw

artist's brush

Can you find these hidden objects?

apple

banana

acorn

butter knife

eyeglasses

spoon

nail

Highlights®

canoe

mitten

bowl

present

sailboat

rocket ship

party hat

Can you find these hidden objects?

spatula

pitcher

heart

muffin

toothbrush

slice of pie

pencil

mushroom

crescent moon

candle

handbell

chef's hat

toucan

tack

sailboat

hoe

magic wand

Can you find these hidden objects?

rabbit

fish

canoe

ice-cream cone

trowel

slice of pie

mug

dolphin

mallet

saltshaker

sock

crescent moon

slice of bread

needle

toothbrush

candle

teacup

sailboat

pencil

spoon

tube of toothpaste

heart

golf club

Can you find these hidden objects?

mop

tube of toothpaste

hockey stick

pennant

peanut

drinking straw

golf club

Can you find these hidden objects?

duck

comb

open book

baseball

snake

nail

flashlight

hammer

coat hanger

needle

shoe

baton

eyeglasses

glove

shoe

fork

heart

elephant's head

Can you find these hidden objects?

cap

tulip

cupcake

artist's brush

banana

fish

mug

ice-cream cone

closed umbrella

Illustrated by Maggie Swanson

spatula

golf club

crown

mallet

musical note

lollipop

nail

Can you find these hidden objects?

needle

fish

shoe

flag

hammer

carrot

candle

clothespin

crayon

toothbrush

Illustrated by Linda Weller

Highlights®

boot

sock

ice-cream bar

comb

cap

nail

Can you find these hidden objects?

fishhook

teacup

pencil

heart

mallet

pie

mouse

COUNTRY MARKET

Illustrated by R. Michael Palan

Diners' Delight

Forks were first introduced in Great Britain 400 years ago.

yo-yo

canoe

kite

banana

flag

crescent moon

Can you find these hidden objects?

sailboat

basket

needle

egg

candle

sock

Highlights®

thimble

candle

carrot

butterfly

wrench

ring

toothbrush

slice of pizza

2 crowns

doughnut

snake

spatula

flyswatter

mallet

golf club

heart

wishbone

eyeglasses

mouse

ladle

ice-cream bar

mug

comb

mushroom

Can you find these hidden objects?

½ OFF

SALE $7.

Sale

March is National Craft Month.

harmonica

bottle of lotion

flashlight

ruler

crown

iron

artist's brush

pennant

Can you find these hidden objects?

snow cone

eyeglasses

heart

sock

ring

toothbrush

tube of toothpaste

Highlights®

feather

canoe

mitten

toothbrush

Can you find these hidden objects?

light bulb

candle

radish

slice of pie

mallet

artist's brush

ballpoint pen

bell

slice of cake

spool of thread

ladder

Red Panda at the Zoo

shoe

musical note

tack

crescent moon

funnel

bird

flashlight

candle

dragonfly

Can you find these hidden objects?

sailboat

polar bear

wedge of cheese

rowboat

loaf of bread

fish

measuring cup

camel

lizard

The National Aeronautics and Space Administration (NASA) was established 50 years ago in 1958.

Blast-off!

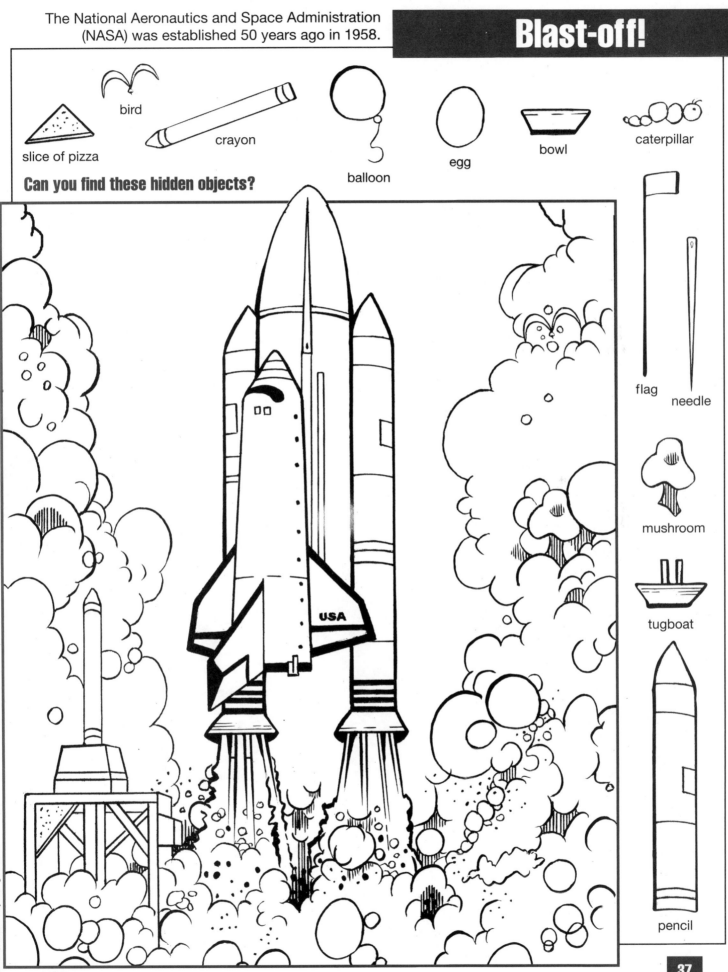

slice of pizza

bird

crayon

balloon

egg

bowl

caterpillar

Can you find these hidden objects?

flag

needle

mushroom

tugboat

pencil

USA

Hayride

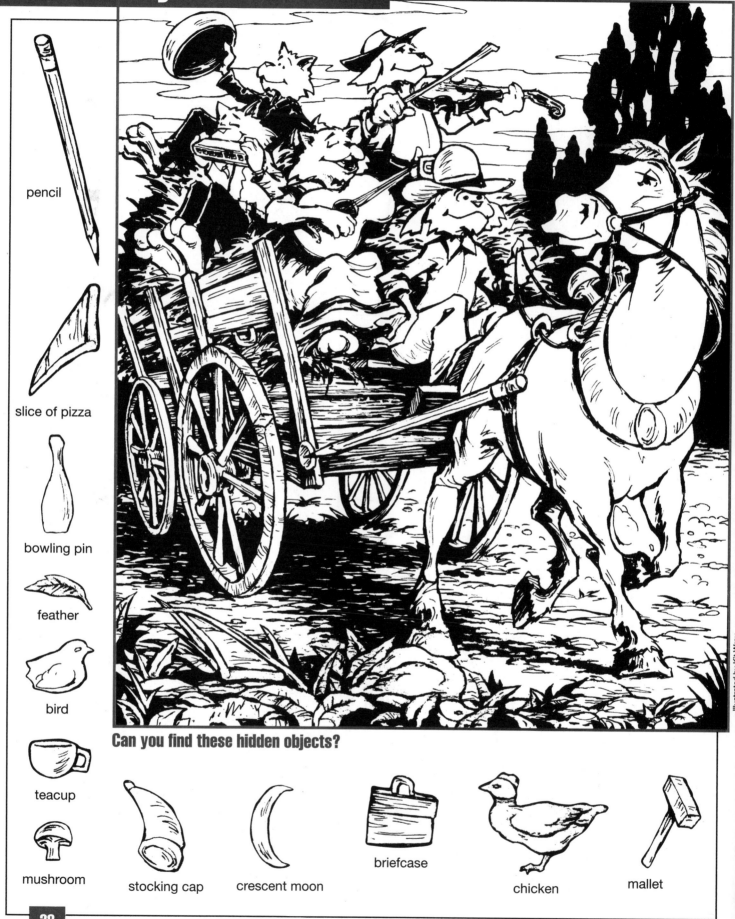

pencil

slice of pizza

bowling pin

feather

bird

teacup

mushroom

Can you find these hidden objects?

stocking cap

crescent moon

briefcase

chicken

mallet

▼Page 1

▼Page 2

▼Page 3

▼Page 4

Answers

▼Page 5

▼Page 6

▼Page 7

▼Page 8

Highlights®

▼Page 9

▼Page 10

▼Page 11

▼Page 12

Answers

▼Page 13

▼Page 14

▼Page 15

▼Page 16

▼Page 17

▼Pages 18–19

Answers

▼Page 20

▼Page 21

▼Page 22

▼Page 23

▼Page 24

▼Page 25

▼Page 26

▼Page 27

Answers

▼Page 28

▼Page 29

▼Page 30

▼Page 31

COUNTRY MARKET

▼Page 32

▼Page 33

▼Page 34

▼Page 35

Answers

▼Page 36

▼Page 37

▼Page 38

▼Cover